Living the Amazing

SEVEN SIMPLE TRUTHS TO
MAKE YOUR HEART BEEP

JACQUELINE S. RUIZ & JUAN PABLO RUIZ

Living the Amazing

© Copyright 2022, Fig Factor Media, LLC.
All rights reserved.

All rights reserved. No portion of this book may be reproduced by mechanical, photographic or electronic process, nor may it be stored in a retrieval system, transmitted in any form or otherwise be copied for public use or private use without written permission of the copyright owner.

Fig Factor Media, LLC | www.figfactormedia.com

Cover Design & Layout by Juan Pablo Ruiz
Printed in the United States of America

ISBN: 978-1-952779-26-8

To Leo and Giullianna

About the Authors

They came to the United States from Mexico and fell in love. He was creative. She was ambitious. He loved beautiful design and fast cars. She wanted to change the world by helping others. Then they made a choice to beat the odds, live the dream, and author their own amazing life. Jacqueline Camacho-Ruiz and Juan Pablo Ruiz have touched thousands through their creative work, philanthropic endeavors and speaking engagements. Amidst many challenges, they built

JJR Marketing, Inc. into one of the top creative firms in the Midwest. Dreaming of what the future can be is an intuitive pastime for both authors. Juan Pablo enjoys drawing his dreams, racing his sports cars and creating designs for JJR clients. Jacqueline uses journaling and meditation to bring her dreams to life. By way of these channels, she leads JJR, founded the *Fig Factor Foundation*, a nonprofit that empowers young Latina girls, and is one of the few Latina sport airplane pilots in the US. Living the Amazing is Jacqueline's ninth book and the first co-authored with Juan Pablo.

Contents

	AMAZING, THE WORD	6
	NOTES FROM THE AUTHORS	10
	HOW TO EXPERIENCE THIS BOOK	14
Truth 01	**A**CTIVATE YOUR PASSION	15
Truth 02	**M**AKE IT HAPPEN	25
Truth 03	**A**CCELERATE YOUR DREAMS	35
Truth 04	**Z**AP NEGATIVITY	49
Truth 05	**I**NNOVATE CONSTANTLY	61
Truth 06	**N**URTURE RELATIONSHIPS	71
Truth 07	**G**ENERATE VALUE	79
	WITH LOVE	84

LIVING THE AMAZING

The Word

AMAZING (adj.): Causing great surprise or wonder.

TO LIVE IS THE RAREST THING IN THE WORLD. MOST PEOPLE JUST EXIST.

-OSCAR WILDE

What is living the Amazing?

When you breathe happiness
When your actions create an energy that propels you forward
When 95% of the things you love are 95% of the things you do
When others lift your spirit higher than the tallest mountain
When your senses feel the wind's kiss and hear nature's music
When difficult days become blessings
When the smallest of things seem brilliantly beautiful

. . . then you are living the AMAZING

Where is this Amazing?

Inside of YOU.
Doing what you love + light-filled +
excitement + 100% feels right + makes your heart
beep + good news all around + magic + giggles + people
reach out to you constantly + great feedback + health + trust
without question + magnetic + confidence + lovely things + ability to
do what you want to do rather than what should do + fully awake + 360°
beauty + deeper connections with others + motivation + wealth + being a role
model for others and elevating them + little moments of depth + a well-lived
life + creativity + inspiration + aware + endless possibilities + YOUR AMAZING
LIFE + anytime inspiration + future is now + feeling complete + little moments
of great depth + feeling alert + living passionately + abundance + joy + ability
to conquer difficult situations with grace + gratitude + inspiring strangers
+ serving others +innovation + creating possibilities + connecting
resources with opportunities + enduring relationships +aligning
with your authenticity + embracing abundance + thinking
bigger and beyond + believing in yourself + expecting
the best + leading others with action +
creating intentionality

Notes From the Authors...

Today. Is. Yours.
Naked like a baby, scattered in a million pieces, a titanium circle of energy that moves you forward, a siren that sings your desires, neat or messy, hopeful or dark – today is yours.

Sometimes, we are so busy "doing" rather than "living" that it's hard to see ourselves as authors of our own story. Life comes at us. Deadlines and meetings. Bills. Bread and milk to pick up. Hustling to sports practices and recitals. Tired. What's for dinner? Bedtime rituals, a full dishwasher to empty, social calendars to live up to, friends who need us, cars on the red letter "E." Sometimes we run on empty too. No gas. Nothing to move us forward.

I get it. When I came to the United States at the age of 14, I felt like my entire life was running on empty.

I sat in the backseat of an old, rusted Chevy Impala, bumping along mile after mile, my mother in the front seat, face stonily looking forward, my brother driving. With my head propped upon my fist, face plastered against the window, my first images of life in the United States were from a distance. The scenes changed like a string of different movies stitched together with green mile markers. I saw snow for the first time in Colorado and sunrises behind mountains in the Gold Mountain Range of hilly Nevada. I saw great cities like Topeka and Chicago with people scrambling around looking like they were in fast forward motion, all going somewhere. There were miles of sleepy Midwest farm towns and cows standing so still I thought they were statues in the open pastures.

NOTES FROM THE AUTHORS

Those cows eked a tiny smile out of an otherwise sulky me.

Just for the record, the odds were not in my favor: a young teenage girl who couldn't speak the language with no money for clothes or history in this place. No roots. I was different than the other kids; I knew that. At 14, different isn't good. But, somewhere in all of that wondering and worry, a little voice inside me whispered: Make something of all this.

So I did. After many stumbles, tears, scratches and dents, I did make something of it. I am a two-time cancer survivor, an accomplished entrepreneur, an international speaker and 10x author, a marketer who has celebrated both failure and success. I am a mother to two good-hearted children. I am founder of a nonprofit that champions young Latinas. I am a devoted daughter, sister, friend and Pilotina (Pilot+Latina).

I found love in this country (thank you, Juan Pablo!). I found success (thank you to all my clients and mentors!). I am living my passions (thank you, Mom and Dad, for giving me wings). I discovered an amazing life. Actually, I live the AMAZING. And I want this for you too.

Living the AMAZING means doing what you love, being excited about your day, and seeing the world with grateful eyes. You believe anything is possible and everything is good. You feel it. Your connections with others run deep and generous like rolling rivers. You are fully awake, aware, alert. You feel complete. And your completeness lifts others up. Money doesn't make this happen. Things don't make this happen. YOU make this happen.

Each day comes with an expiration date: 24 hours come and gone. The sunrise shouts GO, GO, GO! And we choose. Light over dark. Love over hate. Positivity over negativity. Courage over cowardice. A full life over a half-lived life. An amazing life over anything less.

There's that word again: amazing. AMAZING. Using a word with intention empowers us to live the word.

But maybe you haven't heard Amazing's voice for a while. I promise you that after reading this book what might be a murmur will become a thunderous chant so fierce it will make your heart beep. Heart's beep? Yes, I learned this from someone I love very— my beautiful daughter Giullianna. She and I were staring out the window one night. Her soft brown eyes drank in the moon. Her intense look made me wonder what was so special. It was, after all, just the moon. I asked her what she thought of it. She replied: "The moon is so beautiful that my heart is beeping."

I looked at her and realized that what she described was how life *should* feel—*could* feel—if we let it.

Amazing is one single moment. Amazing is a string of moments that make a life.

Your life. Today is your day.

Now go get it,

- Jacqueline Camacho-Ruiz

When Jackie first asked me to coauthor this book with her, I said: "We're 30. What do we know about an amazing life?".

One look from her made me realize I'd made a big mistake. Darn it! That was not the right answer. Then she told me in a quiet voice (which made me nervous because Jackie is always so full of life, like a sparkly fire cracker!) how I completed her and that the two of us had made a life that really was amazing because we had chosen to make it that way. We had done it together. That's why, she said, this book was ours to write.

Sometimes you don't realize where your feet are standing until long after you have traveled there. You don't think about how you got to that point. There's a phrase—"It is hard to see the forest from the trees"—and that is true.

I didn't see how special our little "trees" were in the forest.

Her challenge to me of writing this book made me look at our life with fresh eyes. Thinking about sharing what we knew made me want to hold my family close to me. I looked at my sketch pads and pens like old friends who understood me. I was grateful for the shoes Leo tossed in the middle of the living room, the thousandth interruption of the day to go to the park by Giullianna and even the client who asked me to redo their logo—again.

Suddenly I saw an amazing life that I didn't even realize I had! Sharing it with you then became something I really wanted to do. Because I want you to be happy. I want you to live the AMAZING.

Thank you,

- *Juan Pablo Ruiz*

WHAT IF...

YOU HAD EVERYTHING YOU NEEDED TO LIVE THE AMAZING TODAY, THIS MINUTE, RIGHT NOW?

LIVING THE AMAZING

HOW TO EXPERIENCE THIS BOOK

Most books are expected to be read cover to cover. But *Living the Amazing* isn't like most books. Your reading experience is defined by you and your life. You are invited to go as deeply as you want within these pages.

For instance, there may be chapters that speak to the events in your life today. So, if you have a dream you've wanted to kick into action for a long time, you might find the advice in chapter five, entitled "Innovate Constantly," immediately relevant. Go to it, read it, experience it with all your senses. Or, if you feel like doors are closing more than they are opening, then chapter four, "Zapping Negativity," will be a welcome source of breakthrough inspiration.

However you approach this book, *Living the Amazing* is about finding *your* Amazing in short order. Like life, the way you read this book might mean taking an unconventional path.

Throughout the book, you'll find icons with exercises and ideas for you to do. These *Living the Amazing* prompts will definitely make you think. But if you want to skip over them or do only certain ones, that's your choice as well.

Living the Amazing is your journey to make. Here we go. . .

NOTE: Look for Jackie or JP's icon to read their story.

I. ACTIVATE YOUR PASSION
Imagine all the big things you were meant to do.

Beginnings

For those of us who have walked the dark, shadowy roads of illness—edged with fear and cold-as-ice reality, we know: There is no time to waste. Life was meant to be lived.

Start with your passions.

Passion is a feeling of joy, that heady layer of life where time goes unmeasured. You are aligned with your life purpose. Passion is a force you feel in the center of your heart. Where joy overflows like a river rushing abundantly and deliberately forward. You never question passion. You feel it in every part of you. Your emotional, spiritual and physical selves dance. They sing. Time stops. There is movement coursing through you.

whooshhhhhhh . . . whooshhhhhhh . . . whoos

The rhythm of passion takes you, consumes you, becoming a more and more brilliant light that shines through you.

Passion is that fire in your belly that makes you do things you never thought were in you. Ever.

- *So take that one extra step.*
- *Connect with people in new and different ways.*
- *Open up your heart to the possibilities.*
- *Open up to the universe.*
- *Let your spirit giggle.*
- *Be flexible.*
- *Exude gratitude.*
- *Get all tangled up with joy, just because . . .*

Living with passion is amazing.

I remember the first time the switch inside me flipped. It was the first time I sensed there was something bigger than the things I knew.

I was a little girl and my family was moving from Mexico City to a small town in the state of Aguascalientes, Mexico. I remember reading this book by Zig Ziglar about making a life of success based on how many people you help become successful. I didn't really understand all that he wrote, but something inside—I mean way deep inside me—reset like a switch as my small finger followed each sentence like a bold stripe on a pillow.

Every time I helped somebody, an amazing rush washed over me.

Ziglar's simple message became very vivid for me. I started to discover the deep roots of joy. Real joy. I discovered my passion for making a difference in other people's lives, a passion I honor today.

Easy, right? Maybe if you are a fictional character and someone else is writing your script. Activating your passion is NOT ALWAYS EASY. Sometimes it comes from going down the wrong road. I know. I have traveled down that wrong road.

Two years after starting my business, I learned the value of activating my passion by not following it at all. You might think this is going to be a rainbows and butterfly story, but it isn't. Far from it.

I had long been struggling with the fact that I was a young Latina, an entrepreneur, a mom, and (deep breath) a little on the short side. All those traits didn't fit the stereotype of someone who could walk into a boardroom with high level executives and tell those suits how to market their

I. ACTIVATE YOUR PASSION

company.

I felt like I was faking it. I wasn't being authentic to *me*. I was trying to be someone else. I was trying to live up to the person I envisioned in my head—the tall, confident American businesswoman with years of crystal marketing awards sitting behind her desk chair and a secretary who handed her steaming hot caramel macchiato every morning at a big mahogany desk. The kind of female leader I saw in the movies.

But that wasn't me.

Here's the truth: I didn't embrace that I was a Latina. I was hiding it. I wasn't living my passion. I wasn't being authentic to who I was. You can't live your passion without authenticity. Not ever.

Then came that one game-changing, tear-filled day. I came home after a stretch of meetings, exhausted (it's a lot of work pretending to be someone else!). I looked in the mirror in the little bathroom in our old house (first floor townhome, all of about 1500 square feet). I stared at my image for a long time and said with love and tears in my eyes: *Stop faking it. RIGHT NOW! Embrace yourself for who you are. Jackie, I love you. I love who you are. I love what you represent. I love you exactly the way you are.*

That night I saw my mother in my eyes. I saw my father. I saw all the people who believed in me over the years. And through that experience, I discovered my authenticity. The stereotype in my head disappeared. I tapped into my passion of helping people through *my* talents and the gifts *I* brought to the table—all five feet three of me!

Activate your passion today!

I. ACTIVATE YOUR PASSION

1. Recognize that there is something inside you that is bigger than everything you've ever known before.

2. Believe in your passions, welcome them, hug them, let them run free.

3. Focus on "a life of living" rather than "a life of doing."

4. Be vulnerable: Give until it hurts (just enough to make you feel like you've done something big), mentor a young person, give flowers unexpectedly, forgive someone (you know who—he or she has been hoping for this day), build somebody up, recognize a stranger—say their name and recognize something extraordinary in them.

5. Open up your mind: journal, pick up a book you never thought to read, champion a local cause, talk to someone new.

6. And be kind to yourself. Be patient and reasonable and, above all, be aware.

7. Trust your inner whisper. Run toward the life you were meant to live passionately and beautifully as though it were the only train you ever wanted to catch.

LIVING THE AMAZING

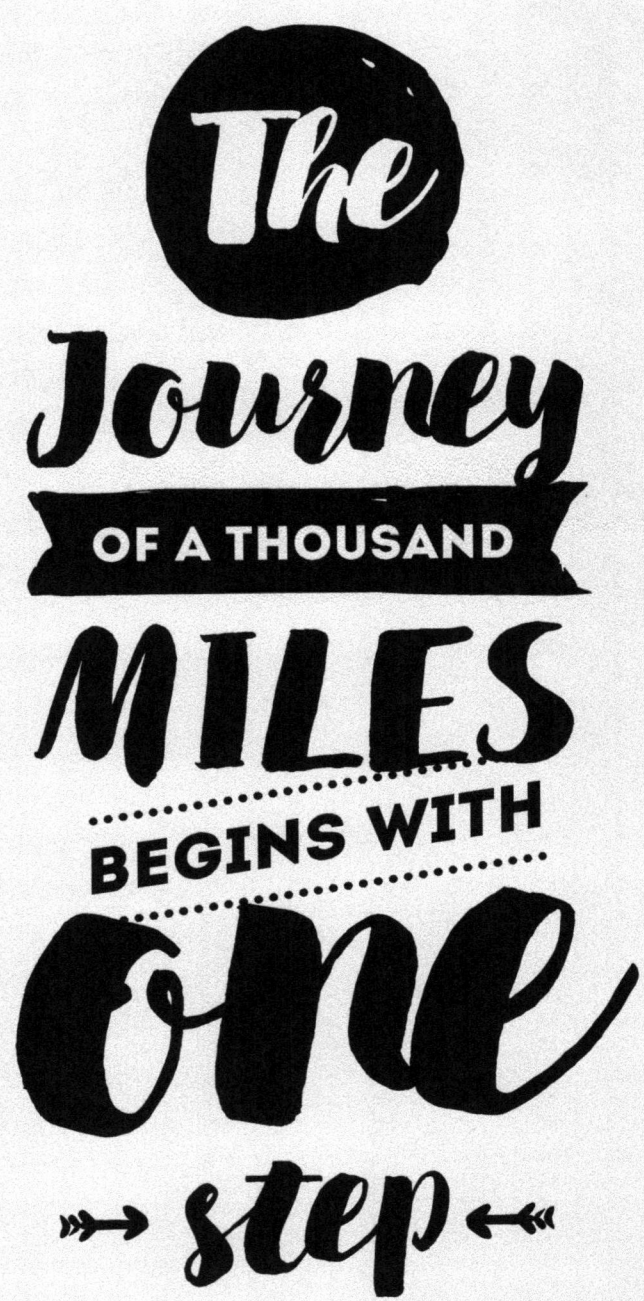

I. ACTIVATE YOUR PASSION

I am a lucky man. I fell in love with someone who showed me how following my passions meant doing the things I love—like expressing myself through design, racing my sport cars and being a caring father.

Men don't normally think about following their passions. We don't think like this. We take care of our families. We are hunters. We are warriors.

Passion, though, has changed the way I live my life. Here is what it means to me.

Passion is waking up every morning knowing you'll be doing something you love the rest of the day. And if that passion is benefiting you and your family, then you have really made it.

I think a lot of people can be blinded and think they have found their passion just because they enjoy doing something. But if that passion is not doing anything good for you, then maybe it is more of a hobby or maybe even something not so good for you. Taking that a step further, if what you are doing is causing issues between you and your family, between yourself and others, then it is not worth it . . . real passion makes the people you love happy too, like a brilliant Van Gogh painting.

Take a second and think about the first time you did something with all your heart and soul. Maybe it was singing or throwing a football or writing a poem.

I remember the first time I felt passionate about something I did. It was the first project Jackie gave me. One of her first clients wanted to do a brochure. Jackie had given the project to another designer, but she was not happy with the results. That moment was the first time I took a step toward something that would later become my life's work.

> MEN DON'T NORMALLY THINK ABOUT FOLLOWING THEIR PASSIONS. WE DON'T THINK LIKE THIS. WE TAKE CARE OF OUR FAMILIES. WE ARE HUNTERS. WE ARE WARRIORS.

I had always seen life through images. But coming to USA as a young man, I put that part of me in a box. My focus was making a living, learning the language and being an accepted into the mainstream. I never thought much about the fact that posters and art and fonts and pictures made me happy inside. The moment my eyes rested on that flyer, I realized that I, Juan Pablo Ruiz, could do something really big with it.

So I picked up the brochure and told her I could do a better job.

PEOPLE WITH PASSION CAN CHANGE THE WORLD.

At that time I wasn't even prepared with a good computer or software. I spent countless hours after work—I was a waiter in a country club at the time—just figuring out how to use the design software we ordered. Then the next morning I finished the flyer . . . we made some revisions between Jackie and I, and then sent it to the client. The client was very impressed. I discovered I could take advantage of a talent I had very deep inside me since childhood.

In art, there are relationships between opposites. Goethe's color wheel is based on opposites using the primary colors of red, yellow and blue. The eye hungers for the opposite of another color so that, together, they live in harmony. So now I share with you the opposite of passion so you know the whole story, so you see a balance as you would see in a beautiful painting.

I was getting tired of working nights, weekends and holidays all the time. That's the restaurant business. I felt the heaviness of not being recognized for what I did, even though I knew I was doing a great job. I think that when people are not recognized, it is very easy to settle into mediocrity. Why try and be good at something when nobody really cares?

Steve Jobs is a great example to me of someone who lived his passion. He pursued beauty and his deep enjoyment of Apple's products. Even when most of his people would only see dollar signs, he saw something much more meaningful, and it transformed millions and millions of people. Jobs wasn't passionate about computer hardware. He didn't live for corporate board meetings. He was passionate about building tools that would help people unleash their own personal creativity. He was a true believer of living with passion. He's famous for this quote:

"People with passion can change the world."

I believe that too.

Activate your passion today!

I. ACTIVATE YOUR PASSION

So here's a little list I made about the shortest road to finding passion...

1. Keep looking, don't settle.

2. Don't measure life by dollar signs.

3. Focus on the things you love and the people those things impact.

4. Learn new things and work toward more goals.

5. There is no limit on how many passions you may have so keep expanding your circle.

6. Take nothing for granted. Giving back to your family or community is the best thing you can do.

7. Good karma will always have your back.

I knew when I was not living my passions. I was spending hours and hours just doing. This taught me something that I will pass on to you now. It's probably the most important thing I can say about passion.

Passionless work is existing, not living.

LIVING THE AMAZING

OPEN UP YOUR HEART TO THE POSSIBILITIES. OPEN UP TO THE UNIVERSE. LET YOUR SPIRIT GIGGLE. BE FLEXIBLE. EXUDE GRATITUDE. GET ALL TANGLED UP WITH JOY, JUST BECAUSE . . .

living with passion is amazing

II. MAKE IT HAPPEN
Let your dreams become the stuff of everyday life.

I would sit near my mother, my eyes wide, chin resting on my tiny fists, watching her in quiet awe. I was not yet ten. She would let me come with her on visits to people's homes. I would carry her bags of cosmetic products she sold. She was my first and greatest example of making it happen.

To me, the phrase leaves excuses in the dust. You know the ones: *I don't have time, we don't have the money, too busy, someday . . . and so on.*

Making it happen means possessing a relentless commitment to the physical manifestation of an action item, goal or dream. Your eye is on the mission – rather than the actions that lead to it. It means not being content until you have accomplished what you set out to do. It is *drive*, not sheer ambition that positions you to obtain the things you want.

MAKING IT HAPPEN = PURITY OF INTENTION

Don't die with an unfinished painting or book or marathon still left inside you. Get your bucket list in order and do it. Before you take another breath, consider the risk of not making it happen. Here's a little poem I wrote just for you...

The way you see
The dreams ahead
Is a vision, beautiful and bold
Images, flickering like sparks in the night
A story aching to be told
Without taking dreams a little further
They are forever left behind
Like smoke that disappears
Grey to nothing, a death cruel and unkind
Into thin air
Into thin air
Don't let your inner hopes disappear
Dream bravely and then "do"
That is the way you see
The dreams ahead, just up ahead
Waiting patiently for you

II. MAKE IT HAPPEN

Want to be in a play? OK. Here's the script.
The play is called:

THIS MOMENT RIGHT HERE, BETWEEN YOU AND ME.

YOU: Great stuff, Jackie, just really great. Nice that you believe all this, but I am buried under a ton of responsibility. You want me to make it happen with all of this "life stuff" going on?

JACKIE: Yes. The simple truth: connect dreams with action.

YOU: I'm listening.

JACKIE: Believe in yourself. First and foremost. If you don't believe in yourself, others will have a hard time believing in you too. And you'll want everyone in your circle to support you as you make it happen!

YOU: I haven't thought about believing in myself for awhile.

JACKIE: Then recognize your gifts and know they are real. Making something happen starts with a thought! You give permission to yourself for an action to take place by thinking of it first. That's how a little baby thought grows up to be a major accomplishment.

YOU: I never thought of it that way.

JACKIE: You CAN make it happen. The best day of the week is today. Right now. Ready for a challenge?

YOU: [Well? What's your answer?] . . .

LIVING THE AMAZING

ONCE YOU MAKE A DECISION, THE UNIVERSE CONSPIRES TO MAKE IT HAPPEN.

- RALPH WALDO EMERSON

II. MAKE IT HAPPEN

JACKIE'S 30-DAY MAKE-IT-HAPPEN CHALLENGE

In the spirit of the Maker Revolution, a contemporary movement of young people who focus on making things using innovation and manufacturing technology, I formally invite you to accept the 30-Day Make-It-Happen Challenge.

Through my work with the Fig Factor Foundation, an organization that empowers young Latinas, I see the wonder and potential in young people. They teach us so much! Here, we are taking their amazing concept of creating innovation and directing its energy toward making things happen for YOU.

Week 1: Press Go!

Mentally prepare yourself to do it, to really make something important happen—however great or small. First, get in the mindset to be confident and creative. Here's what I do. Try some of these ideas or come up with your own:

- Meditate
- Run
- Drink a green juice
- Brainstorm
- Write in a journal
- Listen to your fav song, LOUDLY
- Call someone who you trust
- Share your dream with someone you love
- Create a vision board

Now choose the medium that speaks to you and commit. Set down your dreams. Have you said them out loud, recognized them, given them life? They are real now. Want to visit the moon? Looking for love? Hoping to write your novel? You might not accomplish your dream in 30 days, but this I promise you:

You will be on your way!

Week 2: Climb Bravely

Every little step counts.

Speaking of steps, what are the actions needed to make the amazing happen?

Write them down. Draw them out. Close your eyes and dig a little deeper. Talk to people and get their advice. For every result, there are steps that came before it.

Right before your eyes, the amazing unfolds. You SEE the path. You EMBRACE the journey. You are ON YOUR WAY.

Keep breaking down steps into smaller and smaller action items until you are able to put them in motion.

Want to know a secret? One of the reasons that people don't make their dreams happen is because dreams seem so easily expendable. In other words, you don't have to do them to survive. Dreams won't necessarily pay the bills or get you a promotion. They might do that, but they don't always. Playing a beautiful concerto on a violin may not net you extra income. But, oh, will it make your heart beep if that is your desire.

Week 3: Keep Going!

Too many dreams are lost because someone simply gave up.

WEEK 3 is about endurance and expanding your circle of support. WEEK 3 is pivotal. Here's how you might feel: You don't see results fast enough. You want to quit. You start cleaning the dishes and sleeping in over pushing through.

Push through anyway.

Remember, you are not alone! Think about your circle of people. Your family, partner, friends, neighbors, colleagues at work, clients, children, even strangers all play an important role in you making it happen.

They may be cheerleaders or naysayers (even these people can help if we use their negativity as fuel). Our circle of people help us springboard to making it happen. For example, someone very close to me once questioned my becoming a pilot. She told me she did not want me to leave my children as orphans. I responded confidently, saying, "I am not doing this to die, I am doing this to live." This comment fueled me to prepare as much as I could to become a pilot and to take my actions seriously and intentionally.

Who is in YOUR circle of support for making it happen? In WEEK 3, share with them where you want to go and how they can help. Give your partner a list of what they can do to help you make it happen. Here's my list:

» Support at home
» Delegation of tasks
» Taking care of the children
» Making dinner—unexpectedly
» Purchase items that support my husband's passion

Now write down three ways YOU can help OTHERS in your life make it happen. Here are mine:

» Help the people I meet in business achieve a goal or a dream
» Create an accountability plan with them and be their support
» Celebrate small wins

Week 4: Measure the Amazing

Get ready to feel your heart really beep. Look at the steps you've checked off, the movement you've made toward making it happen. The commitment of others to helping you make it happen. Yes, you did it!!

Making it happen isn't easy. Sometimes, it's very, very hard. Sometimes, you may even feel like the odds are against you.

Earning my pilot's license was that way for me. It was not a priority, a necessity, or an urgency, but . . . it made my heart "beep" with excitement. For me, flying is a spiritual connection. I could have given up months ago. There is so much to learn, so many complex things that defy everything you know about life on the ground. It is a risk, a challenge—but pure beauty and exhilaration all at the same time. To command an aircraft all by yourself (except I do keep a special teddy bear always sitting next to me as I fly!) is something that gives me goose bumps. I fly! Heart beeping!

Beyond the challenge, be confident. Confidence is probably the number one quality that has pushed me beyond the finish line. Confidence is fuel. You can touch it, feel it, see it. Confidence envisions the prize. It allows you to stay focused, committed and ultimately persevere through obstacles.

May these words flow through you...

Pure beauty . . . pure blessings . . .

Allow me to leave you with this short story about something I made happen in my youth.

Writing in my journal in high school redirected my life. I committed to writing in my journal for 365 days, every single day. I did it! I even went beyond the 365 days. I knew that if I could follow-through on that small commitment as a teenager, I could certainly take the same discipline and apply it to bigger things in my life.

SMALL STEPS MOVE US FORWARD. SMALL STEPS LINED WITH LOVE.

It's very clear-cut for me. I'm a guy. Maybe that's it. Many people associate my gender with brevity (I've been accused of being a man of few words more than once!) But, to me, making it happen means getting your job done, and getting it done right even if you tried several times and failed.

I see people rushing to get to things. Rushing down the street, hurriedly walking through the grocery store or sprinting to get off work. It's like the speed of life is getting faster for all of us. I think most of us make it happen all the time but just barely. We are barely living to get by. In fact, many of us seem to be living to work rather than working to live. This makes me want to go on a little adventure.

I want to climb a mountain. When I get to the top, here is what I want to shout:

DARE yourself to do it!

Making it happen is not a walk in the park. There have been several times in my life where making it happen almost didn't happen!

One was when we were trying to publish Jackie's first book *The Little Book of Business Secrets That Work!* We needed to send the files to the publisher and we were under unbelievable pressure. It was just a few days before the big historic book launch event. The printer also needed a few days to print and deliver the books and we were still editing files. It came down to our last weekend. We spent hours and hours, working until very, very late at night. Our kids were desperate for attention and probably hungry as well. We didn't have time to eat, show up as parents or do anything that weekend except get the book ready. By Monday, the printer had the files and the books were in production. They were delivered less than 24 hours before the event. This experience taught me something:

Anything is possible if you keep at it.

Supporting the person you love is a gift.

It's much harder to keep on going, but much more rewarding.

Your family can survive one weekend on nothing but granola bars!

The reason making things happen is key to living the amazing is because action moves us forward. The events, experiences and things we create result from taking action. I believe appreciation from others and for others is the key. The feeling of being recognized can be addictive . . . in a good way. To be encouraged and to encourage others can change a life.

In a marriage, this is not always easy to do. Since that is one of the most important parts of my life, let me just say a few words about it here.

It's kind of rare to have both partners positive about something at the same time. I don't know why this is. We must learn to support the other person and convince the other person that what they want is not silly, that it is achievable, that it is the right thing to do because they feel it in their heart.

Jackie has convinced me to do things sometimes that I didn't like or that I felt were not right for me at the time—but then I look back and I see she was right. She has helped me be the best "me" I can be. Without her support, this would not be. I do the same thing for her.

In life, I believe we are here to show appreciation to all the people in our life. When we show them what they can do or encourage them to step outside their comfort zone, we make a real difference. We help them live a life that is truly amazing—not just for a day or a week, but every day and every week.

I am a father, a creative director, a son, a friend and neighbor. I am a race car driver and artist and chief curator of my children's artwork. Like you, there are many things calling for my attention. Here are the things that put me in the mindset to make it happen. Maybe you can use some of these ideas or they will inspire you to think of new ones that fit your life. . .

II. MAKE IT HAPPEN

DISCONNECT FROM EVERYTHING ELSE.

IF THERE IS NO SACRIFICE, THERE IS NEVER GOING TO BE A CHANGE.

WHEN THERE IS A CHECKMARK CHECKED, THERE IS ONE LESS TO GO.

I see Jackie has a 30-Day Make-It-Happen Challenge. I have a 1-Sentence Make-It-Happen Challenge.

Look at a person who has really made it. Is that person all that smarter than you?

That's it. That's my challenge for you.

Small steps move a person forward. This I believe with all my heart. Here's a personal story I will share with you.

My childhood dream was always to be around beautiful and powerful cars. So I thought maybe I would get a job in the car industry or why not become a car designer?

But, besides spending hours reading car magazines or online blogs, I never took any steps into it. A couple years ago I found out about a place in Joliet, Ill. that has a professional racetrack, and it's also a social club. (I did try golf and other things but none of those things made my heart beep.) I attended the racetrack because I was invited to it by a car dealership and basically fell in love with the place and the lifestyle it represented.

In an exercise we did at one of our quarterly JJR meetings, I said out loud to everyone that I wanted to become a racecar driver. One year later, I was racing at least once a month with my now modified sports car. I'm also a part of amazing car events where I meet other people with the same passion.

The little boy who loved cars so much grew up to actually race them. Sometimes I can hardly believe it. I put myself in that setting so many years ago, and I am so happy to actually be living a passion that has always been inside me.

I really want to leave you on a high note, but Jackie is much better at that than I am. So I'm going to share what I think stands in most people's way of making things happen. My hope is that you will take this and throw it in the garbage. I have and you should too. That way these things won't stand in *your* way any longer.

Say goodbye to . . .

Mediocrity, fear of failure, the comfort of living in "survival" mode.

LIVING THE AMAZING

make it happen

III. ACCELERATE YOUR DREAMS
Living the amazing starts this minute.
Come on, the clock is ticking.

Jan and I walked through a Sedona vortex – nature's hallways that snake around tall cylinders of red rock around which air is said to swirl with healing energy. We absorbed the good and breathed out the grief.

When you are dying, there is something comforting about the hard, cool surface of earth.

I asked her, "How do you feel? How do you feel about your situation, about what you're going through?"

I marveled at how she could be so brave knowing the inevitable. She said, "I am doing everything I can, taking every supplement, every vitamin, eating everything that is healthy for me, and I'm going to live. I don't care what the doctors say. I'm going to live." She has two sons, a husband. She has reasons to want to live.

Later, when the sun was falling, she said, "You know what? I know I'm going to die. But I'm going to make my days here count."

She stopped and looked straight at me, "Because nobody knows when."

Conventional thinking whispers in our ear:

» We can't afford that special trip.
» Life's too busy to see an old friend.
» Someday I'm going back to school.
» We don't have the background for the job of our dreams.
» Or the talent to write the book inside us.
» Or the stamina to run the half marathon.

WHY TRY? WHY NOT?

» Everything begins with a small step.
» When it comes to dreams, go ahead and put the cart before the horse.
» Consider it done. Act as if it is already done. Then walk confidently forward and meet your dream. Embrace it.
» Every day that you don't do something to accelerate your dream, someone in the world is missing out on your inspiration.
» Are you good with that?

I miss you, Jan. This chapter is dedicated to you. ♥

Big dreams, little dreams and does it matter?

I believe there are small dreams and there are big dreams. There are short-term dreams and long-term dreams. I think all of us have an ultimate dream that becomes our LIFE MISSION – our overall purpose in life. For me, it is to serve others in all their dreams.

Accelerate Your Dreams

1. HAVE A VISION.
Write it down, and you're half way there. Create a vision board with pictures and images that connect you with your dream.

2. BE COMMITTED.
The definition of commitment is: something that is important to you but not urgent to the rest of the world. Break dreams down into steps. Put those steps into your calendar. Record your dreams and listen to yourself talking about your dreams.

3. MEDITATE.
I read once that if you can hold the thought of your dream for sixteen consecutive seconds times four—that's a total of sixty-four seconds—then you will manifest that dream. The challenge is keeping the thought alive with life's distractions and interruptions.

4. SHARE YOUR DREAMS WITH OTHERS.
If everybody knows where you are going, they will do everything they can to help you get there.

LIVING THE AMAZING

5. BE A DREAM ACCELERATOR.
Hey, it's not just about you and me in this world. Add fuel to other people's dreams too.

6. DON'T TAKE "NO" FOR AN ANSWER.
Be relentless about your dream. Do something every single day that gets you closer.

7. MAKE SOME NOISE.
Celebrate inside yourself, in your career and with your family. Breathe. You're making your dreams come alive!

8. TAKE IN THE MOMENT.
After the celebratory hoopla, take in the moment when your dream has actually arrived. Not there yet? Recognize milestones along the way. Stop, quiet yourself and wrap yourself in the beauty of having coming this far.

A letter to my children about dreams . . .

Dear Giullianna and Leo,

My biggest and most important dream is to make sure you grow up as genuine citizens of this world—people who are making a difference. People who are incredibly connected to your mission. In that mission, my hope is that you serve other people the way your father and I do.

My hope for you is that you will be authentic, kind and compassionate.

When you see a need, help.
When you hear someone cry out, answer them.
When you notice slumped shoulders, lift that person up.
Live to serve and serve to live.

You are very fortunate living in this country. But, as you know, it is not that way for all children around the world. In our visits to see Grandma and Granpa, you know that there is a lot of poverty in Mexico where I was born. Another dream I have is to help youth by building a center in Mexico where they can find their passion. It's going to be called The Amazing Center. I already have the property donated.

They will go there and have the opportunity to cook, to express themselves, to play sports, to read books, to have music lessons. It will be a place where they can explore a wide variety of talents.

Your dad and I have always believed that what we show you is what you see. Some children don't have museums and libraries and creative outlets to explore. So let's show them a bigger world. Let's show them that they are defined—not by how others see them—but by their own individual dreams.

When dreams define our path, anything is possible. Anything.

Love you to the moon and back,

Mom

Start a list of things you love. You'll feel an energy in every one of those activities and your dreams will race to the top, tripping over each other in a sloppy, happy run to get your attention. Your dreams are bigger than you. When the struggles of life consume you, your focus is on surviving. Of course, you will honor your responsibilities, but don't focus solely on them or you will always be in a constant state of crisis. Control the things within your control — like dreams.

What you focus on will grow. Focus on your dreams.

REALIZING YOUR DREAMS ON EARTH IS LIKE BEING IN HEAVEN.

. . . where you feel complete and one with the universe and God and the rest of humanity . . .

No dream is impossible. Pinkie promise.

When you allow love to guide you and nurture your imagination, you will achieve anything. Love is the greatest force in the universe. You have everything you need inside you to achieve any goal or overcome any obstacle. It is the way you think, your attitude, the love for what you do. It is your love for one another.

III. ACCELERATE YOUR DREAMS

DREAMS COME SLOW AND THEY GO SO FAST.

- Passenger

Oh, sure, Giullianna snuggles on Jackie's lap and yet my beautiful daughter won't put away her toys when I ask her to. On top of that, she gives me the eye. And I think: I'm the luckiest guy in the world. All the men reading this will most likely understand this. And, yes, I think it is as funny as you do.

There's a phrase: "The sky's the limit."

Jackie is a pilot. When I'm flying with her, it seems like every problem or challenge you might have looks so small from above.

Does that give you hope about accelerating your dreams too?

It does for me.

ALL DREAMS ARE NOT CREATED EQUAL. ALL DREAMS ARE, HOWEVER, CREATED TO HAPPEN.

To me, there are realistic and unrealistic dreams. There are big ones and small ones. And it really doesn't matter how they look to the world. It matters how they look to you. When you have dreams you really have a purpose in life. If you feel like you don't have a purpose in life, you might discover it when you are pursuing a dream.

The journey may surprise you!

III. ACCELERATE YOUR DREAMS

A letter to my children about dreams . . .

Dear Giullianna and Leo,

My dream is for your mom and I to leave a legacy. I might draw it out and she might write it out, but we are doing it together. I hope to show future generations—especially immigrants to the United States—that you can be anything you dreamed of as a child. I want you to be anything you want to be. You don't have to come from a wealthy family in order to have better opportunities.

Your mom and I started from nothing. And I hope you do too when you go into the world because from nothing, amazing things happen.

As long as you have passion.

I also dream of traveling the world and experiencing new things (but I'm very happy you are both keeping me grounded for now because I love you very much!).

My dreams are also to create new businesses, invest back in Mexico and continue helping whoever we can to achieve their own dreams.

Most importantly, and you now have to listen very closely to what I say here: Never give up on your dreams. Don't listen to people who tell you that you can't.

If we did it, your mom and I, so can you.

Love,

Dad

WHY DREAMS ARE NOT EASY AND THAT'S OK.

Lionel Messi, the soccer player for the Spanish team Barcelona F.C., was always a very small boy who was told he was not going to make it in professional soccer. At the age of 11, he was diagnosed with debilitating growth hormone deficiency. He had to stick a needle into his legs night after night after night, every day of the week, and this over a period of three years. At 13, Messi convinced his family to uproot their lives in Argentina and move to Barcelona where he'd train for the only soccer team in the world that offered to pay for his treatment. The unity of his family was impacted by this adaptation process and temporarily caused a rift between his parents.

But through the adversity, Messi was able to shore up his ambition, nurture a killer instinct and ultimately become the best soccer player in the world.

Through adversity, one can gain heightened perspective. Goals become clearer. Motivations are defined. Subsequent pain and discomfort is batted down with confidence and determination. No one has an easy ride to the top. This is my little story to show you that tough times are OK.

I see Jackie has outdone me again. She has eight things you can do to accelerate your dreams. I have 5. Oh well.

Give these a try...

Accelerate Your Dreams

1. STAY POSITIVE.
There is so much negativity in our world. What you put your mind to is where you will put your action. Let good things grow in your mind.

2. KEEP GOING.
At times when you are trying to reach a large goal, there are people that are going to say "no." Keep going.

3. PRACTICE PATIENCE.
We all want to achieve our goals *today*. We want the fruits of our labor *right now*, but sometimes the timing isn't right for our goal. Be patient. It will come.

4. BOUNCE BACK.
Throughout our lives, people and situations will throw us off our path. There will be people telling you that you can't do it, and there will be challenges along the way that might make you want to quit. Keep your head up and bounce back.

5. BE HUMBLE.
Let your ego alone. Author Og Mandino wrote: "Never be too big to ask questions, never know too much to learn something new." To live the amazing, you must always learn and grow through life.

III. ACCELERATE YOUR DREAMS

ABOUT THOSE CHALLENGES IN LIFE THAT SEEM SO BIG.

I understand. I have been out of work and not felt good about that. I have worried and not slept. I have been scared about the responsibilities of being a father and a husband and what that really means. I have seen people I know be given the diagnosis of cancer. So all I can tell you is that today is the best time to stop being afraid and dream.

Starting today, move ahead. Don't be one of those people who doesn't dare to dream. Not because you won't fail—because you will, that's life—more because we should live with absolutely no regrets and because you don't want to go through life knowing that you didn't go for it.

What do you think about this quote? It's by Neale Donald Walsh: "Life begins at the end of your comfort zone."

To me, it cannot be more true if you think of life as a journey towards our purpose . . . our true calling . . . the fulfillment of our true potential.

Sometimes, people cling to their comfort zones: afraid to change, afraid to step out, afraid of the unknown. They stay where they feel safe and where they know all the rules of the game.

I still struggle with that one. I can fall easily into my own comfort zone . . . but I have always surprised myself when I take a step outside of it.

Forgiving yourself after a screw-up, especially one that has negative consequences, can be a huge emotional challenge. It probably won't happen overnight. But know there is almost always a new chance to get things right. And if the big mistake you made today helps you do better tomorrow, well, then maybe it isn't so terrible after all. One thing I learned at a Dale Carnegie course was to look at this and say, "What's the worst thing that could happen?" . . . Be objective and soon you will realize your problem looks as small as the little specks you see from a thousand feet up in the air.

Just learn from it. That's really all we can do.

Consider this: movie mogul Steven Spielberg dropped out of high school, re-entered and was placed in a learning-disabled class. Only after moving to a new town and getting into a better school did he graduate. Then he was denied entrance into the film school at the University of Southern California. Twice. In spite of these setbacks he went on to direct some of the biggest blockbusters of all time.

To all the people I have loved, known, seen in the grocery store, passed on the street, never met, never will meet . . .

I don't consider myself to be a motivational type of guy, but I think it's great when you can sit down and listen to people. People like to be heard. Try to encourage others in their dreams by telling them they can achieve even bigger things than what they think. After you've encouraged them, find out how they can start. If they don't know, you can make suggestions, but it's better to let the person figure out the first step themselves so they can be committed to their actions.

III. ACCELERATE YOUR DREAMS

The Dream Accelerator

- Remove everything from your life that isn't contributing to your goals. Put down the digital distractions.

- Work at least 24 minutes per day on your dream. During those 24 minutes, work on different things. Work on you, your family, your health, your dreams. Hand over one minute for every hour in your day. You can spare one minute; I know you can.

- Connect with the right people. Some goals may take ten years if you go at it alone. However, if you get the right people to help you, you can accomplish them much quicker. Most people are afraid to ask for help. I was like that. I was always too proud and thought I could do everything myself. Jackie always told me, "Ask and you shall receive." Oh, brother. Now I have to tell her she was right.

Again.

Children know how to be happy. All they want is to be happy. So they do things that make them feel that way. They do things that make their hearts go beep, beep, beep. I wanted to be an architect when I was a little boy. I loved art. Every line I drew had a purpose. Now I use my talents in my work as a creative director. I wonder sometimes why we don't listen to the child inside of us?

WHY REAL MEN CREATE VISION BOARDS. BUT NOT WITHOUT HEMMING AND HAWING FIRST.

As long as I can remember, Jackie has always had a few journals going. Each one has a different purpose. (She actually lays them all over the house, but I probably shouldn't bring that up here.) I thought it was kind of a childish habit at first, but then I started to see how important it is to capture your ideas and think about them.

One day, Jackie asked me to do a vision board. I was skeptical and thought it was a complete waste of time. She practically dragged me to the dining room table.

"I have work to do," I said. Then I saw the cool coloring books, magazines and books and gave in. It even looked kind of fun. Plus, we were doing this together. We used nice pictures and phrases that reflected our dreams like traveling, houses, cars, clothing, books, etc. and ended up with really nice collages. After we did them we hung them in our closet and looked at them everyday while changing.

A year or so later I told her that we should do a new vision board. She was kind of surprised that I brought it up.

But everything we put on the first one had already become real.

To me, DREAMS start on a white canvas. You start sketching with some crazy IDEAS and then add your favorite COLORS. The more you focus on it, the more it starts to take SHAPE.

In the end, you'll have something you maybe didn't expect but also you'll have something you will love. Why?

Because it's your creation. YOU made it happen.

IV. ZAP NEGATIVITY
Tear down roadblocks. They kill dreams.

Hold on tight, my friend.

Because life stinks sometimes.

And when the "gotchas" happen, you have one choice.

Sing. It. Out.

Confession time. I have stood in the middle of the Rosemont Theater after pouring lots of money and endless hours into an event that was supposed to attract more than 20,000 people. We had fifty show up. Imagine fifty people in a 30,000-square-foot space. It isn't pretty.

Well-known author Michael Gerber was there to speak. (Big name = big price.) I even footed his hotel bill. My staff was there. I bought them lunch. My courage was there because, let me tell you, I needed it to stare at all that empty space.

So when you say you're in debt, your relationships are broken, you lost your job or you are having a relentlessly bad time in your life right now, I get it.

Been there. Done that.

After falling apart more than once, I made a decision. I decided to not let bad things take me down. It doesn't mean I don't have a bad day. It means that zapping negativity is one of the best things you can do long before it sits on the couch and takes over the remote control of your life.

The sooner we accept a negative situation, the sooner we become objective about what actually happened. Did my heart break when the big-successful-going-to-make-a-bunch-of-money-day turned into where-the-heck-are-all-the-people-day? Yes. Did I cry? Right again.

Then I stepped back. I looked at the path and what I saw surprised me. I had partnered with someone who made false promises. I had invested without considering revenue projections. I had fallen in love with a grand idea that was, in the end, just a grand idea.

In other words, I had made some serious missteps. Only by looking at the event objectively could I see the truth.

The sooner we remove the emotion, the sooner we triumph over a bad situation. Technically, this is called emotional intelligence. Realistically, this is called being a lifelong learner.

It's human nature for us to be highly passionate, amazing, unbelievable individuals that get emotionally charged—especially when the situation is close to us. It is easy to react without thinking.

But you have to step back and put your objective lenses on. And when you do, you give Mr. Negativity a run for his money.

I have a friend who is a true servant to the State of Illinois, Linda Chapa LaVia. She has held several different political offices. As you can imagine, she has many supporters and, by way of being in the public spotlight, detractors too. I asked her how she handles negativity. She said, "I step away. I do not respond to something negative in that moment. Words are like swords. You have to treat them very carefully because they are easily misunderstood."

IV. ZAP NEGATIVITY

TAKE ONE NEGATIVE THING IN YOUR LIFE. STEP BACK. LOOK IT IN THE EYE AND ASK: WHY ARE YOU IN MY LIFE, YOU LITTLE STINKER?

It's not all about you. It's not all about me (being a parent is a reminder of this one!). So how do you help others zap negativity?

- Give away your positivity freely and abundantly.
- Offer advice.
- Listen to others and their problems.
- Give a journal and encourage others to write.
- Walk in their shoes. Then tell them what you saw.
- Inspire someone to color, create, do a piece of art, explore a new hobby, reconnect to those things that make them happy, the things that make their heart beep.

The simple act of doing something you love, even if you are living in a moment of negativity, is going to help you get out of it.

We all need role models. Sometimes for different parts of our life. My role model for zapping negativity is . . .
ta da . . .

GIULLIANNA RUIZ
At the time of this writing, my daughter is seven. Her happiness and positivity emits joy and possibility, like a brightly colored piece of music or a spring day infused with heavenly light. She opens my eyes to rainbows and hearts and stars and butterflies and all the beautiful things in life. She is my role model for compassion and giving. Those two things are friends to positivity. Here lies the truth in living the amazing.

Who is Your Role Model for Positivity?

Write a note to that person. Tell them why you picked them.
You will be amazed at what follows.

JOY. BEAUTY. AMAZING.

I love my power words. I feel positivity when I hear them, when I say them, when I write them.

WHAT ARE YOUR POWER WORDS?

"IT'S ALL OF US OR NONE OF US."

My best friend told me this once. I'll never forget it. He's not one to go on and on. But his few words give me strength rooted in unity, compassion, collaboration and love.

I can get through my worst day with his words.

Thank you, Juan Pablo.

REMEMBER MY STORY ABOUT THE ROSEMONT THEATER?

Now I want to tell you about the value of zapping negativity. When you don't give up. When you go at it one more time.

You become stronger, smarter, sharper, faster, happier.

In 2015, I authored my seventh book— *Today's Inspired Latina, Vol. 1*. It is a collection of 27 incredible stories from Latina women in the US. I wanted the book launch to be big so I rented out a prestigious banquet hall with jumbotrons, a wait staff, space for hundreds to gather. I secured a top-of-the-line sound system, stage and lighting crew. We invited media and well-known celebrities and politicians of Hispanic heritage.

We sold out. We have done it two more times for volume 2 and 3 with over 500 people everytime and now planing volume 4.

I was shocked. Do you know why I think this happened? Because the first time I did an event like this it flopped. But that didn't deter me from ever doing it again. I learned from it.

And you can too. You can learn from every experience that bites you in the behind and every time you want to kick a wall because things didn't go your way and every badly broken day.

Step back. Figure it out. Zap negativity like you mean it.

I promise you this:

You will feel Amazing. Your heart will beep.

You will feel energy in everything you do, in the fluctuation of your voice, the way that you stand and the way that you walk, the way you embrace other people and hug them, the words you choose in an email or a voicemail.

This energy and love will infuse everything, from going out of your way to help someone to feeling, crying, loving, yelling and even dancing like a kid at the end of a long workday.

In aviation, the art of flying is really about the art of managing energy. Positivity is also the management of energy. Energy comes from within. The outside world can give cues and ideas to pump up your energy, but it will never give you the source of your energy. Your light is intrinsic. You don't have to climb Mount Everest like explorer George Mallory or traverse the depths of the ocean like Jacque Cousteau or fly to the moon like Elon Musk. The energy is within you to do extraordinary things right here, right now.

DISCOVER, NURTURE, EMBRACE YOUR ENERGY. THEN GIVE IT AWAY.

IV. ZAP NEGATIVITY

TRY THIS:

The day is hot—red flag conditions since mile one. Your tired feet cross the finish line. You hear a voice. That voice is you a long time ago. Before you started the big race, before you knew what PB meant, before you embarked on this challenging journey called life.

What does the voice say? Write down the words and take them with you today.

Faith = Believing in something you cannot see.

Believing in something greater than yourself is to believe that you will achieve it. You will get there.

Believe.

There are a lot of things I don't know, but this I know for sure: Seeing the positive side of things is the key—and knowing that there is a reason for everything, good and bad.

Jackie tells the long version of a story. I don't. It's just the kind of guy I am. I do have a little story though. It's about how I came to be a creative director and a business owner and an amateur racecar driver. None of these things were supposed to happen. I came to this country from Mexico when I was 16. It was all about survival. I never thought I would be anything except someone who survived. But living the amazing is not about the bare minimum.

So here's my little story.

Everything Jackie and I have created would not have happened if we were negative people. None of it. There are always obstacles and people in your life who will bring you down. There are people who look for negativity as if being happy or having nice things is a bad thing. You have to remember that nothing is perfect, but your positive attitude will give you peace and happiness and it will stand guard against the people who try to take these things away. A positive attitude is something you bank. You protect it. You keep it with you.

A good example is how JJR came to be the company it is now. I was very skeptical and negative when Jackie first wanted to start the company because I thought we were too young and inexperienced. I thought we were wasting our time. But somehow her positivity convinced me and we just kept going until, months later, I saw the great potential we both had.

The End

I like to cook. Like my artwork, preparing food in the kitchen is another way to create something that wasn't there before. Here's a little something I cooked up to zap negativity...

IV. ZAP NEGATIVITY

A Recipe to Zap Negativity

INGREDIENTS:

- Perspective
- Worries
- Actions
- Decisions

DIRECTIONS:

1. Put your perspective on the counter. Find the positive parts inside of it. Set those off to the side.

2. Look at the worries that are left. Ask: what is the worst thing that could happen and am I worrying about something unnecessarily?

3. Dump all the unnecessary worries in the trash. Better yet, throw them down the garbage disposal. These are things outside of your control.

4. Focus on the things that you can do something about. They might still be worries, but that's OK because of what comes next.

5. Take simple and focused actions toward those things that really worry you. These are things you can do something about.

> WALK AWAY FROM ANYTHING THAT GIVES YOU BAD VIBES. THERE IS NO NEED TO EXPLAIN OR MAKE SENSE OF IT. IT'S YOUR LIFE. DO WHAT MAKES YOU HAPPY.

Sometimes, you get to help others zap negativity. To me, this is as important as doing it just for yourself. Or at least, you can empathize with them and try to help.

In my experience it's better to stick to light topics when talking to people when they are down. It helps them smile. Negative people tend to sink into "self-victimizing" mode sometimes. One good thing that helps others who are trying to overcome negativity is to praise the person for the positive things they are doing.

As a father, it is very important to always give my children examples of my childhood and try to show them how blessed they are compared to the circumstances Jackie and I came from. Kids nowadays sometimes take stuff for granted. They don't know what it takes to put food on the table or to buy the things they use everyday like electronics or clothes. I think we live in an era where kids are growing very materialistic but don't know how to earn their things. Maybe we as parents are at fault since we try to give them everything we didn't have growing up.

When I look at my life, at the times when I have been most UNHAPPY, it has been when I have focused on "things" rather than "people."

Sometimes giving our children, or even ourselves, less is really like giving more.

"MY ROLE MODEL FOR ZAPPING NEGATIVITY IS . . .

Definitely Jackie Ruiz.

I have not met a more positive person ever. Jackie is the perfect example of somebody who sees the positive side of everything, including people. It's amazing how she can meet someone and see a light very deep inside of them—something bright about themselves that they can't even see.

IV. ZAP NEGATIVITY

Here's a quote about zapping negativity. We keep it by the toilet.

"THE BEST GIFT YOU CAN GIVE OTHERS IS YOUR POSITIVE ATTITUDE."

There are many things to love in life and one of them is failure.

A failure is just another lesson. We wouldn't be good at what we do without failure. Look at Michael Jordan. He always says he is what he is because he failed so many times. So all the worry and all the negative energy you breathe out counts for almost nothing. I say "almost" because it does count as a losing strike. You miss the chance to connect with people you love, you don't see nature, which is so beautiful all around us, and you get stuck in a very forgettable moment. What a trap.

Loving failure, bouncing back and learning from it clears a path.

In the end, going the extra mile is what really counts and does all that other stuff make a difference anyway?

ABOUT THE WHOLE "PERFECT" THING. IT DOESN'T EXIST.

Most of us try to be the perfect parents, the perfect husband or wife, the perfect son or daughter, the perfect worker. Nothing is perfect. Based on my experience, the most valuable moments are those moments that are so simple like spending a Sunday afternoon playing board games with your children or taking a walk with your partner.

These are simple things to do. But they are not easy things to do when you feel a lot pressure or negative things are happening around you. In those times, breathing deep and enjoying the simple things seem really, really hard, almost impossible.

There have been times when I wanted to give up. When negativity felt more natural and more comfortable than positivity. That's when faith comes into play. There is only one way to go when you are at the bottom and that's up. So have faith in God, the universe, others, yourself.

I believe in having faith because with faith and confidence and hope, you have already done something amazing.

LIVING THE AMAZING

A NEGATIVE MIND WILL NEVER GIVE YOU A POSITIVE LIFE

V. INNOVATE CONSTANTLY
You will never regret being bold.

Fearless thinking propels us forward.

Fearless thinking leads to innovation.

Fearless thinking does not mean we're not scared to try.

It just means we won't let the eebie jeebie scaries stand in our way.

First, let's see what we mean by innovation. You might be surprised.

Innovation is, in most cases, not inventing something new. Rather, it's taking something that already exists and putting it in a different context. Steve Jobs didn't invent phones. He revolutionized them (and a few other things). Nicola Tesla didn't invent cars. He did figure out how to make them run without gas. Look at composers, artists, inventors, writers and other innovators from around the world and throughout history.

Everyday people like you and I are innovative too.

An example. At JJR, we produced a deck of cards. Now if you go to Las Vegas, you will see thousands of decks of cards. But you won't see ours. Our colorful and easy-to-read deck highlighted complex marketing tactics. Reshuffled, you could instantly see the impact various marketing channels could make on your business.

Like most innovation, though, it didn't stop with what we had created. Many times, innovation replicates itself. It gets bigger.

I used the cards at the *Small Busines Week* celebration hosted by *Crain's Chicago Business*. People loved their simplicity. One person approached us to do an app version. Four of our clients adapted the cards for their vertical businesses.

Switching gears, can we innovate within our own families? Short answer: yes. In fact, you just stumbled on a big part of living the amazing. Now I'm going to show you why.

Many people in business are familiar with core values and positioning statements. Imagine creating core values and a mission statement at the kitchen table.

Pretty amazing, actually.

My friend and colleague Michele has been doing this with her family for years. Her children Katherine, Patrick and Peter are now teens on up. On their kitchen wall is a piece of paper with three columns. Each column is titled with a different value and ideas to build them out: "volunteer for jobs nobody else wants" is listed under Go for Great, "do one big family event" is under Embrace Family, and "walk in another's shoes" is cited under Live the Faith. Family dinners touch on examples and failures. The list is always up.

Most importantly, when each person is not in the safety net of the family home, these values organically race to the top. As these values show up so does the family's innovation to honor them: bringing a dinner to a neighborhood family experiencing illness, writing in a family faith journal, assigning mentoring roles from one sibling to another, joining a school volunteer group that works with the community.

Now, it's your turn...

V. INNOVATE CONSTANTLY

THINK OUTSIDE THE BOX

WRITE YOUR FAMILY POSITIONING STATEMENT.

What makes our family different?
What do we stand for?
Why is this important to us?

WRITE YOUR FAMILY VALUES.

What are the core values of our family?
How can we bring our values to life?
Why are these beliefs important to us?

There's always a better way to do things, a better way to solve issues, a better way to innovate. We are constantly bombarded with noise in our community and in the world. Consider this:

It is challenging to set aside time to capture ideas that will make our lives better. But pausing to think about how we can make things better is a bold act of innovating. Why not innovate constantly? Why get stuck in our ways? Why not grow? Why not drive it forward?

"I DO."

Can a married couple be innovative? Yes, yes, yes. It's amazing. Let's infuse the intimacy of marriage with the collaboration of ideas and thought. Commit to innovation as a couple.

» challenge one another
» admire one another's good ideas
» research together
» invite the other person to do something new
» ask: what are your stretch goals?

Every couple of weeks, Juan Pablo and I sit down and talk about ideas, our future, finances, dreams, products we're going to create, where we are going in our life, and how we are going to make the next mile marker. We brainstorm. That's innovation as a married couple – supporting, listening and encouraging each other.

Now I hand the dry erase marker to you. All you need is your partner and a whiteboard.

V. INNOVATE CONSTANTLY

. . . IF YOU LEAVE WITH NOTHING ELSE, KNOW THIS: TAKE NOTHING FOR GRANTED . . .

Look at a chair in a room. Just pick one. It defies gravity. It doesn't fall down. It is solid, useful, beautiful, comforting. How did something so physical manifest from a thought?" How does it seamlessly flow with our movements? For me, it's a way of thinking. Whatever your field is—whether you're marketing beauty products or funerals or natural foods—there is an opportunity to cultivate the extraordinary in ordinary things.

Objectivity makes the biggest difference.

If you can see an opportunity with objectivity, you see your options. You don't settle for just one. If you have high debt, don't look at the numbers. Be innovative. Look at all your options to conquer debt: an extra job, financial discipline, a zero percent credit card, budgeting strategies. Lead with innovation.

If you want to become an author, don't look at words not yet written. Be innovative. Look at the story you want to tell, share the idea with your spouse or best friend, set a word count goal each week, do some research. Begin to write.

These are your passions—things you want to accomplish. Innovation makes them achievable.

Speaking of innovation . . . Juan Pablo and I are big fans of modernist furniture. We like the clean lines and simplicity. Nobody sells more of this style than IKEA. The company's founder Ingvar Kamprad is described by best-selling author Malcolm Gladwell as "a rare breed — he possesses a combination of conscientiousness, openness, and disagreeableness. These personality traits are what made him a fearless innovator in the beginning of his career."

Are you a fearless innovator? Of course you are. It's already inside you.

There's always a better way and if you use your **curiosity**, listen more than you talk, and ask good and thoughtful questions, you'll get to the core of the issue so you can **create** something beautiful.

Status. Quo. Defied.

LIVING THE AMAZING

Obstacles to Innovation

NO TIME

NO SUPPORT

PEOPLE WILL THINK YOU'RE CRAZY

YOUR OWN LIMITING BELIEFS

"IT'S NOT GOING TO WORK"

"I HAVE NO MONEY"

"WHO AM I TO INNOVATE?"

NOT BELIEVING IN YOURSELF

FEAR NO ONE WILL LIKE IT

QUITTING BEFORE IT'S DONE BECAUSE OF PREVIOUS FAILURE

NOT TAKING ACTION

TOO BUSY

Fuel to Innovate

HANG OUT WITH INNOVATORS

HOST THINK TANK SESSIONS

BRAINSTORM YOUR IDEAS

MIND-MAP YOUR IDEAS

ASK MR. GOOGLE

RESEARCH PROJECTS

READ INTERESTING CASE STUDIES

APPLY FOR INNOVATION PROGRAMS

BREATHE DEEPLY

GO SOMEPLACE COMPLETELY DIFFERENT

TAKE A CHANCE ON BEING GREAT

SAY THE POSSIBILITIES OUT LOUD

V. INNOVATE CONSTANTLY

JUST US

It's just you and me here. I feel your eyes on this page looking for answers. I implore you: Do what makes your heart beep. In any innovative project I've been involved with, it all started with making my heart beep—that incredible feeling of love and joy inside my heart that becomes the beneficiary of a divine download. You know the spark. It's that idea you can't get rid of, that begs you to take a step and then another until your dream manifests itself.

An inspiration is an idea begging you to do everything you can to make it happen. When that tug shows up, kick into innovator mode.

> "IF I HAD ASKED PEOPLE WHAT THEY WANTED, THEY WOULD HAVE SAID FASTER HORSES."
>
> - HENRY FORD

For me, personal innovation is rethinking the ways you do things on a daily basis and improving them each passing day. Maybe you have applied some personal development into your life, but as the times change, what got you successful before might not work for the future. Time is not like a painting where it just stands still. By making a commitment to personal innovation and evolving yourself, you make yourself a better person than you were yesterday, a month ago, or a year ago.

Innovating constantly is the only way to achieve dreams and keep the success that you already have.

"I DO."

Innovation doesn't happen by accident. Neither do amazing marriages. Apply the same principles of innovation to your partner to make the relationship stronger and stronger as time goes on.

THE NEXT BEST THING MIGHT BE IMPORTANT SO WHY ARE YOU WAITING?

A few years ago, I focused a lot on print design rather than digital or web designs. I was skeptical to go into digital simply because it wasn't the direction I wanted to go. As demand grew in our company, I had no choice but to accept it and learn more. I read books, spent days and weeks trying out digital design options and pretty soon I was building websites on my own. To this day, websites and digital newsletters are a great source of our marketing business income. I wished I had chosen to innovate earlier and faster.

Here are my tips for you:

» **Prepare to disagree. Come up with your own ideas and ignore the naysayers.**
» **Make a promise to grow yourself.**
» **Practice vision. See the best person you can be. What does he or she look like? Are you eating better? Are you closing deals as a business owner? Are you happy? What's in that vision board?**

THE BIG FIGHT: CREATIVITY VS. INNOVATION

I hear this a lot: creative people are innovative. I disagree. Creativity is the capability or act of conceiving something original or unusual. Innovation is the implementation of creative ideas. They may be very similar but I think anybody can be creative and come up with new or different ideas. But it takes a heck of a lot of courage and heart to take action.

Really, there is no innovation until something gets implemented.

Many creative ideas will die a slow death because someone didn't do something about them.

Elon Musk of Tesla and SpaceX fame is a good example. He says, "Failure is an option here. If things are not failing, you are not innovating enough." I like how he ties innovation with solutions for our future, whether its renewable energy solutions, transportation, or vacation packages to Mars.

To me, personal innovation is not being satisfied. Personal innovation is about making yourself better at whatever it is you do. If you have happy customers, ask for feedback and think of

V. INNOVATE CONSTANTLY

ways to really wow them even more. If you are successful, go beyond where you are today. It's easy to accept whatever life gives you or the way you grew up.

I was that way. As an immigrant to this country, I once thought that I couldn't possibly catch up to those who had lived here all their lives. But that wasn't true. Those were my own limitations I put into place. Once I got rid of them, I was free to imagine what life could be.

Innovation is one of the most important opportunities to move from one social, economic or cultural status to another. Well, you can forget about all that if you want. Maybe that doesn't mean anything to you, and that's OK too. But what about this: innovation is a way to go from satisfied to really happy in your life.

Isn't that a great place to be?

I draw for a living (my children will tell you I color for a living). Here's a tiny feast I put together just for you about innovation...

LIVING THE AMAZING

be the game changer

LIVING THE AMAZING

VI. NURTURE RELATIONSHIPS
People alter our journey in blue-sky ways.

2 People, 2 Stories, 2 Lessons About Relationships.

There are two different people and two different stories about how relationships have led me to living the amazing, a place where I taste life like a person enjoys the heady richness of chocolate.

One story is about a beautiful lady named Irene Anzola, a teacher's assistant in the ESL (English as a Second Language) program in my high school. I was fourteen years old when I met her. It happened to be around the time my father returned to Mexico. I shared with Irene that I was thinking about following him back to my hometown.

Boy, did I hear it.

Irene stopped what she was doing. Her deep brown eyes looked at me, they took all of me in with a yearning that I had never seen before. She said, "Jackie, you can't go back to Mexico. Stay here. You're going to create so much success right here. You have something really special to offer the world."

I was stunned. She saw in me that which I had not yet seen in myself. Her firmness erased the thought of returning to Mexico from my mind. I didn't know why she was right, but I had no doubt that I needed to listen. What she was telling me was to believe in myself, believe in my own potential.

I am so happy I did because that outcome has led to the life I live today. If I had left, I would not have connected with all the amazing people I have met over the past 20 years.

Thank you, Irene Anzola.

The second person is Brian Marshall. He gave me a scholarship to his Sales Without Selling program. While other people were paying $10,000 to attend, I was given a full scholarship. Something I said made him believe I would make something of myself with his course.

Brian changed my life, changed the way I looked at business, changed the way I connected with other people by nurturing relationships and giving without expecting anything genuinely. To this day, I have that implanted in my heart.

I remember him telling me, "Don't base your worth on the money you have in the bank. That has nothing to do with you." It's so easy for entrepreneurs to say, "I'm failing. I'm not worthy" if we are not making as much as we think we should, but money is only one measurement. I know many people who live the amazing life, and money is of no consequence to them. (Just look at children. They are our greatest example of living the amazing! They gravitate to what makes their life happy without even knowing it, and money means nothing to them.)

Thank you, Brian Marshall.

Those two things: believing in myself and giving without expecting anything has helped me in living the amazing.

WHAT'S YOUR RELATIONSHIP STATEMENT?

A mission statement is a great plant-your-flag-in-the-ground proclamation meant to define a collective vision and purpose for a business. Today, I challenge you to write your own relationship statement, a few sentences about your worldview of what relationships mean to you. Here's mine as an example.

I will look at each individual as someone of beauty and goodness in this world. I will live to serve and serve to live. I will close out my day by doing something that impacts another person's life.

VI. NURTURE RELATIONSHIPS

20 Ways To Nurture Relationships

01. PHONE CALL
02. NOTE OF "JUST BECAUSE"
03. THOUGHTFUL GIFT
04. ASK A THOUGHT-PROVOKING, OPEN-ENDED QUESTION
05. COMPLIMENT
06. HUG
07. SHARE A DEEP LOOK
08. GIVE A GOOD LISTEN
09. BIRTHDAY OR ANNIVERSARY REMINDER
10. NICE LUNCH OR DINNER
11. WORD OF COMFORT
12. SUPPORT FOR A DREAM
13. SHOW UP. BE PRESENT.
14. THOUGHTFUL SUPPORT
15. SEND A SONG
16. POWERFUL CONNECTION
17. STRATEGIC OPPORTUNITY
18. GIVE A WARM WELCOME
19. NOTE OF LOVE OR THANKS
20. AN ARTICLE OR BOOK THAT GIVES SOMEONE KNOWLEDGE

Sometimes I feel so much appreciation that my heart beeps extra beeps! I am so grateful to all the people who have helped me get where I am today, to this place of feeling so complete. I record voice messages and send them via text and say: *I just want to thank you for being in my life and for who you are*. When I see them months later, they will often remember those little gestures. Amazing.

NOT EVERYONE IS FOREVER

Sometimes people pass through our life. Sometimes just for a moment.

Big secret: When it comes to nurturing relationships, it doesn't matter how long someone stays in our life. What matters is what you do with that person when they are there.

We are all equipped with this beautiful intuition. Sometimes I know that people come in and out because that's what they need to do. Sometimes they come into our life just to teach us a lesson. That's hard because I want to cling to people who are not meant to stay in my life for a long time. Maybe they are meant to teach you something about yourself or about life so you don't make mistakes again. I appreciate that and embrace that. You can't be close to everyone in your network, but you can appreciate everyone and nourish the relationship that exists today.

Living the amazing is rooted in relationships. Of course, there is one kind of relationship that hovers above the rest: marriage. Here's what I do to live the amazing with Juan Pablo.

I proactively support his dreams. I actively make his day special. We have a lot of small moments throughout the day. We ask deeper questions. We laugh together. We plan together. We have transparency and authenticity. We have regular dates. We connect and recalibrate our dreams. We are thoughtful.

VI. NURTURE RELATIONSHIPS

WHEN IT COMES TO RELATIONSHIPS, EMBRACE THE ENCOUNTERS...

Encounters are memorable, meaningful, all-in touch points. Think coffee with a friend you haven't seen in ages or a conversation where you invest 100 percent of your attention. Phones are off. Worries are checked at the door. Your mind is devoted to the other person.

In contrast, transactions are one-and-done. Think about the question "How are you?" and not waiting for an answer. Or consider the meetings you've had, only expecting to get the business, serve the customer or "show up" for the task you were hired for.

Guess which approach advances relationships? Encounters, every time. Guess which one makes you feel whole and happy? Encounters again. It could be one message—one little message like "I was thinking about you" or "I'm going to be in the area, let's get together" or "I picked up this gift because it reminded me of you."

Relationships are rooted in today.

So make today count.

Make an impact on someone's life today!

"IF A RELATIONSHIP IS FOUNDED ON LOVE, IT DOESN'T END."

- ROSANNE CASH

A little story about relationships...

I think Jackie knows so many people that she could write a whole book on relationships (and probably will!). But I am more quiet so I see the world through a different lens. When I think about relationships, I think of the person who first taught me about what a relationship really means. I am speaking here of Jackie and me. We have been supporting each other in the good and the bad moments just like we promised on our wedding day. It has not been an easy journey or been without the usual husband-wife disagreements. Our relationship is not perfect.

What we do different is that we try to solve our problems the fastest possible way based on communication and coming to a solution together. Our respect and love for each other always wins. We constantly put our pride and ego aside and are tolerant of the other person's way of thinking.

In the first few years of our marriage, I kept to myself a lot. I guess that's how I grew up. Then Jackie showed me a different way of living—sharing my thoughts, goals, problems and anything that should be said. I learned that even asking for help or giving someone something without them expecting it deepens the bond between two people.

Every good thing you do in a relationship makes it grow. From that moment on, it is never the same. It is better, richer and stronger.

MY RELATIONSHIP STATEMENT

It's funny but, when difficult times come, sometimes you see the people who really care about you. **In good times, it's easy to be surrounded by many people. My hope is to always be that person who really cares—who shows up in good times and bad for others.**

ON MARRIAGE

Making your marriage amazing is not easy, but there is definitely ways of making it that way.

Communication and intimacy are key. Take your partner on dates and remember the time when you were only dating. Dates are probably more important now that you have committed yourself to that special person.

Never stop celebrating your anniversary. You don't have to spend a lot of money but acknowledging the day and its importance will remind you of the commitment you have made and show your children that your relationship is important.

Don't be afraid of working or starting a business with your wife or husband. Jackie and I always get the question of how in the world can we work together and still be married after all these years. I really don't get it. Marriage means working with your spouse in life. Business, then, becomes just another opportunity to see that person in a different light.

VI. NURTURE RELATIONSHIPS

TECHNOLOGY AND TIME

I never thought I would sound like my parents, but here I go. It's easy to spend a lot of time on Facebook. We've all done it. Connecting with others more directly, however, is different. I love technology. It's important to my work. But sometimes it just takes over.

Put phones and other devices aside when sharing activities with people. Talk or, even more importantly, listen. It's sad to see people at a restaurant having a "family" dinner when parents and kids are on their phones and pretending to be "connected" when they are really "disconnected."

ONE LAST THOUGHT: MYTH VS. REALITY

There is no "behind every great man, there is a great woman" or "behind every great woman, there is a great man." That's a myth. Instead, work side by side with people.

It's the only way.

10 Ways To Nurture Relationships

01. KIND, CONSTANT AND HONEST COMMUNICATION

02. WILLINGNESS TO WORK THROUGH DISAGREEMENTS

03. A SENSE OF HUMOR OR SOME DISTRACTION FROM DAILY ROUTINE

04. SHARING LIFE LESSONS

05. EMOTIONAL SUPPORT WHEN THINGS DON'T GO WELL

06. NOTICE THE SMALL THINGS ABOUT OTHERS

07. SHARING LIFE GOALS, DREAMS

08. COMPASSION AND FORGIVENESS

09. SHARING NEW EXPERIENCES TOGETHER

10. ADMIT MISTAKES AND TALK ABOUT THEM

LIVING THE AMAZING

MANY PEOPLE WILL WALK IN AND OUT OF YOUR LIFE. BUT ONLY TRUE FRIENDS WILL LEAVE FOOTPRINTS IN YOUR HEART.

- Eleonor Roosevelt

VII. GENERATE VALUE
Can we measure an amazing life?

Can we measure an amazing life?

Good question, right? I mean, how do you really know you're living an amazing life and generating value from it? WHERE'S THE RROOF????

After all, fitness tracking devices measure just about everything: our steps and sleep, body mass and blood glucose, saturated fat and standing hours, water consumed and calcium absorbed. Many of us are obsessed with measuring.

The good news is that the value you generate is inside of you. You are the ultimate measuring device. You don't need technology. You just need you.

Here are a few questions that can help you find answers.

Rate these from 1 (lowest) to 10 (highest). Then evaluate the numbers.

- How loud does your heart beep?
- Have you done what you love—in the last seven days?
- Are you making an impact on one person's life daily?
- Do you feel a sense of abundance in your life?
- What steps are you taking to advance your dreams?
- Are you energetic about your life?
- Are you a magnet of opportunity?
- Are you happy and do you feel complete?
- Do you breathe happiness?

THE VALUE FROM LIVING THE AMAZING EXTENDS TO THOSE WE LOVE.

Here's what you will pass on to your children...

- Energy
- Magnetism
- Vitality
- Connections
- Passion
- Success
- Abundance
- Opportunities

And your life partner...

Living the amazing with your life partner is the fulfillment of your dreams as supported fully by your spouse. You give everything and you receive everything as one gives and receives a gift. In so doing, you have a sense of completeness, abundance and happiness.

VII. GENERATE VALUE

Your Amazing Life

Living an amazing life means **loving** what you do. It means **discovering** your value in correlation to other people's lives and how you impact them. It's a sense of **completeness** and a sense you are living your passion every day. And you know when you are living the amazing because you are purely and wholly **aligned** with your thoughts. You reach a state you've always hoped, one where you can finally say that **you don't need anything** anymore. You have everything, amazing life included. You feel good. You look good. People feel your energy. And you are acutely aware of theirs. You bring measureable **value** to the lives you touch. They are better because of you. Yes, this is living the **amazing**. And it is available to you every second, every minute of every day.

BUT HOW DO YOU REALLY KNOW YOU ARE LIVING THE AMAZING?

You will know when you get there. No one else can tell you the answer to this question. You will know when you see the impact you are making. You will do this by instinct. You will look for ways to give back, to make a difference, to share your happiness like it's a big box of crayons and you want to give them all away.

Since I draw, I see life through pictures. What does your amazing life look like? What is that picture? When you have the picture in your mind, do you get excited about the possibilities? Does your heart feel differently? Mine does.

It's like a circle of energy.

What we are talking about here is success, but not in the sense that most people think. You might consider money or a corporate title when you think of success. But those are only two examples. For most of us, success comes in different shapes and sizes. When setting goals in life or in business, we need to look at what success means to us personally—so when we succeed we will know what it looks like. It's not your job to live up to someone else's idea of success. Your accomplishments and successes belong to you and you alone.

Measure success by your ruler. Measure it by the value you generate.

I think many people measure success according to their bank account. I think this is a big mistake because, when you have a job or a business that's giving you a lot of money but you are not enjoying what you do, can this ever be called success?

Are you living the amazing?

Here are 4 quick questions to ask yourself (I see my little quiz is much shorter than Jackie's):

1. Do you have a passion for what you do?
2. Am I making progress on my life goals?
3. Do I have free time to enjoy a hobby or hobbies?
4. Am I making an impact on others?

There is a lot to teach our children about living the amazing. The two big things I can think of are:

» Generosity in abundance. If we are at a point where abundance is common, and we have received more than what we need, its important to share with others.
» Gratitude despite the circumstances. In life, we will always see ups and downs. Let's teach our children to be grateful even in the hard moments and learn from every lesson in life.

There are a lot of people in our lives. Marriage, however, is the ultimate duet. Two people striving to make a life. Like Jackie and I. That's really what we've tried to do—to make a life we can be proud of and our children can be proud of. Whoever that life partner is for you, inspire each other to become the best you can be. (If you don't have that person in your life, then maybe you have a best friend or someone who puts your priorities on a similar level as theirs.) It should never be one person or the other having all the success or pains. Together, face adversity, set and work toward goals—both personal and as a couple—and celebrate the results. Celebrate the amazing.

One last thing about living the amazing ...

- Do what you love.
- Be positive.
- Be thankful.
- Find ways to zap negativity.
- Eat healthy.
- Enjoy family time.
- Most of all, be yourself. Because that is the most amazing thing you can do in life.

> LIVING THE DREAM IS SIMPLY A FORM OF LIVING OUT YOUR PASSION, OF MAKING THAT PASSION GRADUALLY, THROUGH PERSISTENCE AND EFFORT, A CENTRAL PART OF YOUR LIFE.
>
> - URIJAH FABER

WITH LOVE...

See the world through a different lens: create opportunities, see the beauty amidst hardships, embrace good times with gratitude and extend positivity to every interaction you have, be brilliant and innovate, connect the possibilities when others don't see them.

Cherish your beeping heart.

With love,

- *Your Amazing Self*

www.ingramcontent.com/pod-product-compliance
Lightning Source LLC
Chambersburg PA
CBHW041236240426

43673CB00011B/358